BRAZIL: HUMAN RIGHTS

EXECUTIVE SUMMARY

Brazil is a constitutional, multi-party republic. In 2010 voters chose Dilma Rousseff as president in elections widely considered free and fair. Civilian authorities maintained control over security forces. Security forces committed some human rights abuses.

The most significant human rights abuses included poor and at times life-threatening conditions in some prisons, sex trafficking of children and adolescents, forced labor, and exploitative working conditions.

Other human rights problems included excessive force and unlawful killings by state police; excessive force, beatings, abuse, and torture of detainees and inmates by police and prison security forces; prolonged pretrial detention and inordinate delays of trials; judicial censorship of media; government corruption; violence and discrimination against women; violence against children, including sexual abuse; social conflict between indigenous communities and private landowners that occasionally led to violence; discrimination against indigenous persons and minorities; violence and social discrimination against lesbian, gay, bisexual, and transgender (LGBT) persons; insufficient enforcement of labor laws; and child labor in the informal sector.

The government continued to prosecute officials who committed abuses; however, an inefficient judicial process delayed justice for victims and perpetrators of human rights violations.

Section 1. Respect for the Integrity of the Person, Including Freedom from:

a. Arbitrary or Unlawful Deprivation of Life

The federal government or its agents did not commit politically motivated killings, but unlawful killings by state police occurred. In some cases police employed indiscriminate force. In a few instances, civilians died during large-scale police operations, mainly in the favelas (poor neighborhoods or shantytowns). Credible reports indicated that state police officials continued to be involved in revenge killings and intimidation of witnesses who testified against police officials. Police often were responsible for investigating charges of torture and excessive force carried out by fellow officers.

In Rio de Janeiro there were reports that both on- and off-duty police employed indiscriminate use of force. These acts often occurred in the city's approximately 763 favelas, where an estimated 1.4 million persons lived, according to the 2010 census by the Brazilian Institute of Geography and Statistics (IBGE). The Rio de Janeiro Public Security Institute, a state government entity, reported that from January to July police killed 197 civilians in "acts of resistance" (similar to resisting arrest) in Rio de Janeiro state, compared with 263 during the same period in 2012. Most of these deaths occurred while police were conducting operations against drug-trafficking gangs operating in Rio's poor communities. A disproportionate number of the victims were Afro-Brazilian under 25 years of age. Nongovernmental organizations (NGOs) in Rio de Janeiro questioned whether all of the 197 victims had truly resisted arrest, contending that police continued to depend on repressive methods.

On June 24, the Special Police Operations Battalion entered the New Holland favela within Rio de Janeiro in pursuit of criminals. The operation resulted in a gunfight that left 10 dead, including at least two residents who were not implicated in criminal activity and Sergeant Ednelson do Santos.

In another case Rio de Janeiro resident Amarildo de Souza went missing after officers from the Police Pacification Unit (UPP) operating in the Rocinha favela brought him in for questioning on July 14. Family members claimed the police were responsible for his disappearance; other Rocinha residents alleged that police offered them money in exchange for false testimony casting suspicion on drug traffickers. In September the Public Ministry charged 10 UPP police officers, including commanding officer Major Edson Santos, with torture, murder, and hiding the body of de Souza.

The Sao Paulo State Secretariat for Public Security reported that state military police killed 239 civilians from January to June, compared with 251 in the same period in 2012.

In April a court sentenced police officer Carlos Adilio Maciel Santos from the Seventh Military Police Battalion in Rio de Janeiro to 19 years and six months in prison for the 2011 killing of Judge Patricia Lourival Acioli. Four other military police officers were already tried, convicted, and sentenced while the six remaining defendants continued to await trial dates.

b. Disappearance

There were no reports of politically motivated disappearances.

c. Torture and Other Cruel, Inhuman, or Degrading Treatment or Punishment

Although the constitution prohibits such treatment and provides severe legal penalties for its use, reports of torture and other cruel treatment by police and prison guards occurred. In July the UN Subcommittee on Prevention of Torture expressed concern about the use of torture by security forces.

A Pernambuco state judge released Paraiba state military policeman Gleson de Campos Pereira on bail under partial house arrest to await sentencing from a state court. Campos Pereira was arrested in Pernambuco on charges of torture during the apprehension of four persons suspected of robbery in 2011.

As of November the National Justice Council (CNJ) had not updated its website with the results of its most recent 2012 and 2013 prison inspections. Previous reports indicated evidence of torture and cruel, inhumane, and degrading treatment in prisons.

Prison and Detention Center Conditions

Conditions in many prisons were poor and sometimes life threatening, but many states made efforts to improve conditions. Abuse by prison guards continued to occur at many facilities. Poor working conditions and low pay for prison guards encouraged corruption.

Physical Conditions: Overcrowding was a problem. According to a Ministry of Justice report, as of December 2012 there were 548,003 prisoners – 512,964 male and 35,039 female prisoners – incarcerated nationwide in a system designed for approximately 310,690. An estimated 36 percent of all detainees were awaiting trial. Of the total prison population, approximately 34,000 were under 18 years of age.

The states of Rio de Janeiro and Sao Paulo and the Federal District provided separate prison facilities for women; elsewhere, according to the Catholic Church's Penitentiary Commission, women occasionally were held with men in some facilities.

Federal prisons and state detention centers in the state of Sao Paulo faced severe overcrowding. Government data showed that correctional facilities in the state were 87 percent over capacity and nearly one-third more crowded than in the previous four years.

Frequently prisoners who committed petty crimes were held with murderers and other violent criminals. Authorities attempted to hold pretrial detainees separately from convicted prisoners, but lack of space often required holding convicted criminals in pretrial detention facilities. Many prisons, including in the Federal District, attempted to separate prisoners based on crimes committed to separate violent offenders from nonviolent ones and to keep convicted drug traffickers in a wing apart from the rest of the prison population.

The law stipulates that juveniles should not be held together with adults in jails, but this was not always respected. Multiple sources reported adolescents jailed with adults in poor and crowded conditions. Insufficient capacity in juvenile detention centers was widespread.

In Piaui state alone, inmates killed seven fellow prisoners in the first half of the year. The CNJ considered Anibal Bruno, located in Pernambuco state, the worst prison in the country. Despite receiving 26 million reais ($11.2 million) in public funds for improvements and the construction of new facilities, it continued to face severe overcrowding, with 5,234 prisoners in a facility designed for 1,448.

Prisoners had access to potable water, but sanitary conditions were often inadequate and facilitated the spread of disease. HIV and tuberculosis prevalence rates in prisons were far higher than rates for the general population.

Administration: Recordkeeping on prisoners was adequate. The National Justice Council set up an online database during the year to monitor prisoners' cases and time served, but this system did not always function properly.

Authorities used alternatives to sentencing for nonviolent offenders. Individuals sentenced to less than eight years in prison had the option to serve in "semi-open" conditions, whereby the individual could work during the day and sleep at the prison facility at night. The CNJ found, however, that thousands of prisoners sentenced to semi-open facilities, served their sentences in "closed," or high-security, facilities.

According to Sao Paulo authorities, one-third of prisoners eligible to work did so.

Prisoners and detainees had access to visitors. Human rights observers reported that some visitors complained of screening procedures that at times included invasive and unsanitary physical exams. Prisoners could observe their religious practices and could submit complaints to judicial authorities. State-level ombudsman offices and the federal Secretariat of Human Rights (SDH) officials also monitored prison and detention center conditions.

Independent Monitoring: The government permitted monitoring by independent nongovernmental observers, including the International Committee of the Red Cross. During the year the CNJ conducted prison inspections in 14 states, although it did not make its reports publicly available.

Improvements: After a four-year review of more than 413,000 prisoners' cases, in 2012 the CNJ announced it had freed more than 36,000 prisoners who had been unlawfully remanded to detention and recommended the transfer of more than 72,000 prisoners to reduced security conditions in accordance with federal sentencing guidelines.

In September the state of Paraiba announced that its three main prisons would feature exclusive wings for LGBT prisoners. The Secretariat for Prison Administration adopted the measure to diminish sexual and physical violence against gay and transgender inmates.

Alagoas state finished construction of a new prison in Craibas, designed to include dedicated cells for disabled inmates.

d. Arbitrary Arrest or Detention

The law prohibits arbitrary arrest and detention and limits arrests to those caught in the act of committing a crime or arrested by order of a judicial authority; however, police at times did not respect this prohibition.

Role of the Police and Security Apparatus

The Federal Police, operating under the Ministry of Justice, is a small, primarily investigative entity and plays a minor role in routine law enforcement. Most police forces fall under the control of the states, where they are divided into two distinct units: the civil police, performing an investigative role, and the military police, charged with maintaining law and order.

Despite its name, the military police do not report to the Ministry of Defense. The law mandates that special police courts exercise jurisdiction over state military police except those charged with "willful crimes against life," primarily homicide. The police often were responsible for investigating charges of torture and excessive force carried out by fellow officers, although independent investigations increased. Delays in the special military police courts allowed many cases to expire due to statutes of limitations.

The Brazilian Association of Investigative Journalism reported that police tactics, including excessive force, rubber bullets, and tear gas, resulted in injuries to hundreds of individuals, including at least 15 journalists during June 13protests in Sao Paulo.

According to the Rio de Janeiro State Secretariat for Public Security, human rights courses were a mandatory component of training for entry-level military police officers. UPP officers for the favela pacification program received additional human rights training. Under the pacification program, the Rio de Janeiro State Secretariat for Public Security inaugurated six new UPPs during the year, for a total of 34. As of September, 8,592 UPP officers were responsible for patrolling approximately 226 favela areas in Rio de Janeiro state.

In Rio de Janeiro's favelas, so-called militia groups, composed of off-duty and former law enforcement officers, often took policing into their own hands. Many militia groups intimidated residents and conducted illegal activities such as extorting protection money and providing pirated utility services. Human rights observers believed that militia groups controlled up to one-half of Rio's favelas.

Former Alagoas police officer Edgelson Ribeiro Guimaraes and 10 other members of an illegal militia group, arrested in mid-2011 for committing murders in the states of Pernambuco and Alagoas, were freed on bail awaiting trial, but Ribeiro Guimaraes was arrested again on August 22 for alleged involvement in a robbery in Pernambuco. He was later cleared of the robbery charges but remained in prison awaiting trial for homicide.

Arrest Procedures and Treatment of Detainees

With the exception of arrests of suspects caught in the act of committing a crime, arrests must be made with a warrant issued by a judicial official. Officials must advise suspects of their rights at the time of arrest or before taking them into custody for interrogation. The law prohibits use of force during an arrest unless the suspect attempts to escape or resists arrest. According to human rights observers, some detainees complained of physical abuse by police officers while being taken into custody.

Authorities generally respected the constitutional right to a prompt judicial determination of the legality of detention. Detainees were informed promptly of the charges against them. The law permits provisional detention for up to five days under specified conditions during an investigation, but a judge may extend this period. A judge may also order temporary detention for an additional five days for processing. Preventive detention for an initial period of 15 days is permitted if police suspect that a detainee may leave the area.

The law does not provide for a maximum period for pretrial detention, which is decided on a case-by-case basis. Time in detention before trial is subtracted from the sentence.

Defendants arrested in the act of committing a crime must be charged within 30 days of arrest. Other defendants must be charged within 45 days, although this period may be extended. The backlog in the courts often resulted in extending the period for charging defendants.

Bail was available for most crimes, and defendants facing charges for all but the most serious crimes have the right to a bail hearing. Prison authorities generally allowed detainees prompt access to a lawyer. Indigent detainees have the right to a lawyer provided by the state. Detainees also were allowed prompt access to family members.

Pretrial Detention: Despite constitutional protections, CNJ inspectors found that authorities improperly or illegally detained thousands of individuals. Approximately 200,000 of the country's 550,000 prisoners were in pretrial detention status. In some cases individuals waited years for a court to rule on the merits of their case.

e. Denial of Fair Public Trial

The constitution provides for an independent judiciary, and the government generally respected judicial independence. Freedom House stated that corruption within the judiciary, especially at the local and state level, remained a serious concern, and the judiciary was often subject to outside influences.

Although the law requires that trials be held within a set time, the nationwide backlog in state and federal cases frequently led courts to dismiss old cases unheard. There were millions of backlogged cases at the state, federal, and appellate courts. For defendants and victims, it could take years for the system to hold criminal perpetrators accountable for their actions.

Trial Procedures

The right to a fair public trial as provided by law was generally respected. NGOs reported that in some rural regions – especially in cases involving land rights activists – the perception existed that police, prosecutors, and the judiciary were more susceptible to external influences, including fear of reprisals. Investigations, prosecutions, and trials in these cases often were delayed. After an arrest a judge reviews the case, determines whether it should proceed, and assigns the case to a state prosecutor, who decides whether to issue an indictment. Juries hear cases involving capital crimes; judges try those accused of lesser crimes. Defendants enjoy a presumption of innocence and have the right to be promptly informed of charges, to access government-held evidence and confront and question adverse witnesses, to present their own witnesses and evidence, and to appeal verdicts. Defendants generally had adequate time and facilities to prepare a defense.

While the law provides for the right to counsel, the Ministry of Justice stated that many prisoners could not afford an attorney. The court must furnish a public defender or private attorney at public expense in such cases, but staffing deficits persisted in all states.

Political Prisoners and Detainees

There were no reports of political prisoners or detainees.

Civil Judicial Procedures and Remedies

Citizens can bring lawsuits before the courts for human rights violations. While the justice system provides for an independent civil judiciary, courts were overburdened with backlogs and sometimes subject to corruption, political influence, and indirect intimidation. Cases involving violations of an individual's human rights may be submitted through petitions by individuals or organizations to the Inter-American Commission on Human Rights (IACHR), which in turn may submit the case to the Inter-American Court of Human Rights.

f. Arbitrary Interference with Privacy, Family, Home, or Correspondence

Although the law and constitution prohibit such actions, NGOs reported that police occasionally conducted searches without warrants. Human rights groups, other NGOs, and the media reported incidents of excessive police searches in poor neighborhoods. During these operations police stopped and questioned persons and searched cars, residences, and business establishments without warrants.

Section 2. Respect for Civil Liberties, Including:

a. Freedom of Speech and Press

The law and constitution provide for freedom of speech and press, and the authorities generally respected these rights. The independent media were active and expressed a wide variety of views with minimal restriction, but nongovernmental criminal elements continued to subject journalists to violence because of their professional activities. Despite national laws, politically motivated judicial censorship remained a problem within local-level courts. Some NGOs stated that press freedom declined during the year, citing increased instances of violence against journalists, mainly in the context of the massive demonstrations that shook the country in June and July and drew equally large-scale responses from security forces.

Violence and Harassment: The Brazilian Association of Radio and Television Broadcasters (ABERT) continued to report cases of imprisonment, aggression, censorship, and failure to respect freedom of the press. Between October 2012 and September 30, ABERT reported 136 cases of censorship, threats, direct violence against journalists, and other forms of pressure against news organizations and professionals. ABERT linked 105 of these cases to the numerous protests that occurred since June.

The SDH oversees the Program to Protect Human Rights Defenders, where threatened human rights activists, including journalists, can be placed under government protection. Eight states had their own programs (Bahia, Minas Gerais, Espirito Santo, Pernambuco, Rio de Janeiro, Para, Rio Grande do Sul, and Ceara). The federal government administered the program for states that lacked a program.

Within six weeks, gunmen allegedly killed two journalists in Ipatinga, a town of 250,000 inhabitants in Minas Gerais state. On March 8, assailants shot and killed

Rodrigo Neto, a journalist who worked for a local newspaper, while he was in his car. On April 18, gunmen also shot and killed photojournalist Walgney Assis Carvalho while he was fishing. At the end of November, authorities held 16 individuals, including civil policemen, in connection with the killings. Both Neto and Carvalho had reported on organized crime, specifically the formation of murder-for-hire death squads composed in part of off-duty policemen. In a March 19 visit to Minas Gerais state, Minister of Human Rights Maria do Rosario encouraged a full investigation of Neto's killing. Within one week of Carvalho's death, the state government replaced the Ipatinga chief of police as well as the civil police regional delegate. The Minas Gerais chief of Civil Police stated Carvalho had refused protection.

Censorship or Content Restrictions: The National Association of Newspapers, Brazilian Association for Journalism, and Inter American Press Association regarded the most serious threat to press freedom to be the growing number of cases of judicial censorship of the media. The NGOs noted the continuing trends of the media's dependence "on the political authorities at the state level" and court censorship orders.

Beginning in 2009, Fernando Sarney, son of federal senator Jose Sarney, repeatedly took the *Estado de S. Paulo* newspaper to court to prohibit the publication of reports linking him to official corruption, money laundering, and organized crime. In May the Fifth Civil State Court upheld censorship of the newspaper.

Nongovernmental Impact: During the year unidentified assailants killed at least six journalists, some apparently for their reporting. On June 11, unidentified gunmen shot and killed Jose Roberto Ornelas de Lemos, the director of the *Hora H* newspaper, who had reported on crime and corruption.

Internet Freedom

There were no government restrictions on access to the internet or credible reports that the government monitored e-mail or internet chat rooms without appropriate legal authority. Nevertheless, several legal and judicial rulings had the potential to threaten freedom of expression on the internet. A continuing trend was for private individuals and official bodies to take legal action against internet service providers and providers of online social media platforms, such as Google, Facebook, and Orkut, holding them accountable for content posted to or provided by users of the platform. Judicial rulings often resulted in the forced removal of content from the internet, and Google reported a 265 percent increase in content removal requests during the last half of 2012.

The electoral law regulates political campaigns on the internet. The rules prohibit candidates from buying advertising space online and restrict online campaign presences to websites operated by the candidate.

The International Telecommunication Union and the Center for Information and Communication Technologies Studies reported that 50 percent of the population used the internet and 40 percent of households had access to the internet in 2012. Only 10 percent of homes in rural areas had access to the internet, while 44 percent of homes in urban areas had access.

Academic Freedom and Cultural Events

There were no government restrictions on academic freedom or cultural events.

b. Freedom of Peaceful Assembly and Association

The law provides for freedom of assembly and association, and the government generally respected these rights.

Freedom of Assembly

During countrywide protests in June, security forces used rubber bullets, pepper spray, and tear gas against violent protesters, but in general security forces respected the right of peaceful protesters to freedom of assembly. Security forces occasionally used excessive force on peaceful protesters, particularly during protests in early June in Sao Paulo. In mid-June the federal government met with some protest group organizers to anticipate security needs for future protests, protect peaceful demonstrators, and limit violence.

c. Freedom of Religion

See the Department of State's *International Religious Freedom Report* at www.state.gov/j/drl/irf/rpt/.

d. Freedom of Movement, Internally Displaced Persons, Protection of Refugees, and Stateless Persons

The constitution provides for freedom of internal movement, foreign travel, emigration, and repatriation, and the government generally respected these rights. The government cooperated with the Office of the UN High Commissioner for Refugees (UNHCR) and other humanitarian organizations in providing protection and assistance to refugees, asylum seekers, and other persons of concern.

In Sao Paulo an estimated 20 Sao Paulo businessmen from the Syrian-Brazilian community provided 19 immigrants fleeing unrest in Syria with housing, financial support, and translation services; traditional immigrant support groups, such as the federal government's National Committee for Refugees, also provided assistance. The government provided documentation to new arrivals.

Protection of Refugees

Access to Asylum: The law provides for the granting of asylum or refugee status, and the government has established a system for providing protection to refugees. At year's end an estimated 4,690 refugees from approximately 79 countries were living in the country. From January to July, 1,600 immigrants requested refugee status. The UNHCR's country representative projected a total of 2,500 new refugees during the year, an increase from the 2,008 refugees granted asylum in 2012.

Temporary Protection: The government provided assistance to Haitian migrants who entered the country in hope of securing employment and relief from economic conditions in Haiti. The Haitians traveled through other countries in the region and requested asylum upon entering Brazil. The government did not find that the immigrants warranted refugee status but provided most of the more than 4,000 Haitians with humanitarian visas. The visas entitle them to receive health and social assistance, the right to work, and the right to remain for up to five years. The government also issued a special work visa through its consulate in Haiti for up to 1,200 persons a year to reduce the number of Haitians seeking entry through more dangerous migration routes.

In August at least 40 pilgrims who came to Rio de Janeiro for the World (Catholic) Youth Day requested asylum. The pilgrims claimed they were fleeing violence and religious persecution in their homelands of Pakistan, Sierra Leone, and the Democratic Republic of the Congo.

Section 3. Respect for Political Rights: The Right of Citizens to Change Their Government

The law provides citizens the right to change their government peacefully, and citizens exercised this right through periodic, free, and fair elections based on universal suffrage. Military conscripts may not vote.

Elections and Political Participation

Recent Elections: In the 2010 national elections, which were considered free and fair, Workers' Party (PT) candidate Dilma Rousseff won a four-year term as president.

Participation of Women and Minorities: The law requires that at least 30 percent of the candidates registered by each political party be women, and most parties complied with the requirement. According to the Supreme Electoral Court, there were 3,968 female candidates in the 2010 elections, compared with 15,504 male candidates. Thirteen women were elected to the 81-member Senate and 44 women to the 513-member Chamber of Deputies. Of the 27 governors elected, two were women. Two of the 11 Federal Supreme Court justices were women.

In local elections held in 2012, a total of 7,648 women were elected to municipal councils (gaining 13 percent of the seats), and 663 female mayors were elected (12 percent of all mayors). There were 419,633 female council candidates, representing 32 percent of all candidates.

There were 44 Afro-Brazilians in Congress (one senator and 43 deputies) and one Afro-Brazilian each in the cabinet, Federal Supreme Court, and Superior Court of Justice. Joaquim Barbosa, the only Afro-Brazilian Supreme Court justice, began a two-year term as chief justice in 2012. Indigenous people's participation in politics was mostly limited to the local level.

Section 4. Corruption and Lack of Transparency in Government

The law provides criminal penalties for official corruption, but the government did not always implement the law effectively, and officials frequently engaged in corrupt practices with impunity. There were numerous reports of government corruption. During protests in June, corruption was one of the most widely cited concerns expressed, especially in regards to public spending on venues for the 2014 FIFA soccer World Cup and the 2016 Olympics.

Corruption: In November the Supreme Court remanded 17 of 25 individuals convicted in the Mensalao anticorruption trial to prison. Those incarcerated included former senior officials in the administration of former president Lula da Silva, including his chief of staff and PT president.

The Supreme Court also convicted two sitting members of Congress for corruption-related crimes. In June the court sentenced Congressman Natan Donadon to 13 years in prison on corruption-related crimes. In August the court remanded Senator Ivo Cassol to four years in semi-open confinement for procurement fraud.

On July 4, Congress passed law 039/2013, which creates civil and administrative penalties for Brazilian entities and legal persons that attempt to bribe foreign officials or engage in corrupt practices in Brazil or abroad. Individuals found to have engaged in such acts cannot win government contacts.

According to press reports, approximately 200 of the 594 members of Congress have had criminal cases before the Supreme Court, many for alleged acts of corruption.

Federal government entities such as the Federal Court of Audits, Federal Comptroller General, Public Ministry, Federal Police, judiciary, Department of Revenue and Control of Financial Activities, and Federal Treasury are responsible for fighting corruption. The agencies identified public spending as a source of financial corruption.

Whistleblower Protection: The law protects public servants but does not apply to employees at private companies. Public sector employers are prohibited from disciplining or terminating whistleblowers' employment.

Financial Disclosure: Public officials are subject to financial disclosure laws, and officials generally complied with these provisions. The Office of the Comptroller General serves as the executive branch agency mandated to monitor and verify disclosures. The Federal Court of Audits and the National Judicial Council, respectively, verify financial disclosure statements of employees in the judiciary and legislature. The Federal Revenue Office also can provide a public employee's asset declaration if that person is under investigation for illicit enrichment. While asset declarations are not made public, federal employees' salaries and payment information are posted online and can be searched by name. Such information became available on the government's transparency website when the new Law on Access to Public Information went into effect in June.

Public Access to Information: The law provides for public access to unclassified government information. The list of exceptions is sufficiently narrow and includes personal information; information that affects public safety or health, national security, or international relations; and sensitive military and intelligence information. The only fees charged are the costs of printing, copying, and mailing documentation. The government office has 20 days to respond to requests and can request an additional 10 days, for a maximum total of 30 days, after receiving the request. Agencies responded with full information 78 percent of the time within 11 days. Employees are subject to administrative sanctions for noncompliance and criminal charges if found to have fraudulently or deliberately destroyed or withheld information.

Section 5. Governmental Attitude Regarding International and Nongovernmental Investigation of Alleged Violations of Human Rights

A number of domestic and international human rights groups generally operated without government restriction, investigating and publishing their findings on human rights cases. Federal officials were cooperative and responsive to their views. Federal and state officials in many cases sought the aid and cooperation of domestic and international NGOs in addressing human rights problems; for instance, the Ministry of Labor (MTE) partnered with the International Labor Organization (ILO) to formulate national strategies for combating forced and child labor.

Government Human Rights Bodies: The Secretariat for Human Rights is an office under the presidency that holds ministerial-level rank. The secretariat has jurisdiction over issues regarding persons with disabilities, LGBT persons, the elderly, children, and government representation in international and regional human rights fora in conjunction with the Ministry of External Relations. The Chamber of Deputies and the Senate had human rights committees that operated without interference and participated in several activities nationwide in coordination with domestic and international human rights organizations. Marco Feliciano's appointment in March as president of the Chamber of Deputies' commission on human rights sparked controversy because of racist and homophobic comments he had made in the past, as well as his support for a law that would allow mental-health professionals to treat homosexuality as a mental disorder. Most states had police ombudsmen, but their accomplishments varied considerably, depending on such factors as funding and outside political pressure.

The National Truth Commission, established in 2011, continued its investigations into alleged human rights abuses committed from 1946 to 1988. Commission members met regularly to discuss progress on their specific areas of research. At a May seminar commemorating its first year of work, the commission released a formal progress report and demonstrated a prototype of the online application containing primary documents used by the commission to accompany the release of the final written report, due May 2014. Due to the volume of documents and witness testimony that still required analysis, the commission requested an extension of at least six months.

In July Pernambuco state's Truth Commission, in its first year of existence, reported the investigation of 51 cases of deaths and disappearances dating back to the military government. In two of these cases – including the case of Father Antonio Henrique, whose body was found with signs of torture in 1969 – the commission reached a provisional finding that the deaths were politically motivated.

Section 6. Discrimination, Societal Abuses, and Trafficking in Persons

The law prohibits and penalizes discrimination on the basis of race, gender, disability, or social status, but discrimination continued against women, Afro-Brazilians, indigenous persons, and LGBT persons.

Women

Rape and Domestic Violence: The law criminalizes rape, including spousal rape; sentences for convictions range from six to 30 years in prison. Domestic violence remained both widespread and underreported to the authorities, due to fear of retribution, further violence, and social stigma. The law stipulates a penalty of three months to three years in prison for persons who commit domestic violence, and authorities generally enforced the law effectively. Official statistics regarding the number of prosecutions and convictions were not available.

The federal government continued to operate a toll-free nationwide hotline for women. In 2012 the hotline registered 732,468 calls reporting domestic violence, 11 percent more than in 2011. Calls to the hotline leveled off after an initial surge, which government officials attributed to greater awareness among women of the hotline program. According to hotline data, 57 percent of the complaints received in 2012 concerned physical abuse. An international hotline service enabled Brazilian victims of gender-based violence to call in from Italy, Spain, and Portugal. In the first six months of the year, the international service received 90 calls, resulting in 33 women receiving assistance abroad.

In March President Rousseff launched the 265 million reais ($114.2 million) "Women, Living Without Violence" initiative to improve service to victims of gender-based violence. The program aims to increase the capacity of the women's hotline, provide more public health-care options for women, and construct 27 women's centers throughout the country that integrate specialized police, judicial, prosecutorial, health, employment, and other ministerial resources.

In January the Pernambuco State Technical Chamber for Combating Violence against Women began operations as part of a statewide public security initiative. The chamber is responsible for monitoring and reporting monthly to the governor all actions taken to promote the eradication of violence against women.

In April the Espirito Santo State Court of Justice and the city of Vitoria distributed a "panic button" device to 100 victims of domestic violence as part of the municipality's protection program. The device can send an alert with the victim's exact location to a monitoring center and also capture and record conversations that can be used as evidence in court.

A report by the Rio de Janeiro Public Security Institute revealed an increase in the number of reported rapes in the state. According to the report, from January to July there were 3,453 cases, compared with 2,928 during the same period in 2012. Authorities attributed the increase partly to victims' increased willingness to report assaults.

The Sao Paulo State Court of Justice created three new special courts of domestic and family violence against women. As of September the state of Sao Paulo had a total of 10 special courts to deal with domestic violence. As of July the courts had considered 35,959 cases, mostly related to threats of violence, rape, and coercion. There was no information available on the number of prosecutions or convictions.

Each state secretariat for public security operated police stations dedicated exclusively to addressing crimes against women. The 381 stations provided psychological counseling, temporary shelter, and hospital treatment for victims of domestic violence and rape, as well as criminal prosecution assistance by investigating incidents and forwarding evidence to courts. There were also 218 reference centers and 77 temporary women's shelters operated by state and local governments. The Secretariat for Women's Policies reported that fewer than 10 percent of municipalities had a dedicated space for the protection and care of victims of gender-based violence.

The Secretariat for Women's Policies published the Third National Plan on Women's Policies in August. The plan's main focus was to address gender inequality through public policies that promote the economic, cultural, and political autonomy of women in order to eradicate extreme poverty and enable full participation in society. The Secretariat for Women's Policies acted as the coordinating agency for all actions carried out under the Third National Plan and evaluated the end results across government organs.

The law requires health facilities to contact the police about cases in which a woman was harmed physically, sexually, or psychologically to collect evidence and statements should the victim decide to prosecute.

The Chamber of Deputies' Special Office of Women's Promotion remained active. The office undertakes surveys and studies on the situation of women, specifically pertaining to gender-based violence; works with international organizations and NGOs to share best practices; and heads a network of protection for victims of gender-based violence in conjunction with NGOs, state, and local governments. In March the Senate approved the creation of its own Special Office of Women's Promotion.

A study on gender-based violence (GBV) published by the Institute for Applied Economic Research reported that between 2009 and 2011, the country registered nearly six killings for every 100,000 women. The states of Espirito Santo, Bahia, and Alagoas had the highest levels of GBV-related killings, with 11 deaths per 100,000 women. The study also compared data on GBV-related homicides before and after the 2006 passage of the Maria da Penha law to reduce domestic violence and found that GBV rates had remained stable since 2001.

Sexual Harassment: Sexual harassment is a criminal offense, punishable by up to two years in prison. The law encompasses sexual advances in the workplace or educational institutions and between service providers or clients. In the workplace it applies only in hierarchical situations where the harasser is of higher rank or position than the victim. The government generally enforced sexual harassment laws effectively. No official data were available on the prevalence of sexual harassment in the workplace, but in a survey conducted by the Sao Paulo Secretary's Union, 25 percent of secretaries in the state claimed to have been sexually harassed by their supervisors.

Reproductive Rights: Couples and individuals have the right to decide the number, spacing, and timing of children and had the information and means to do so free from discrimination, coercion, and violence. Access to information on contraception; skilled attendance at delivery; and prenatal, postpartum, and essential obstetric care generally were available. According to the 2013 UN Population Fund report, skilled health personnel assisted in 99 percent of births.

Discrimination: The cabinet-level Secretariat for Women's Policies supervises a special entity charged with overseeing the legal rights of women. Women's labor force participation (75 percent) was below that of men (85 percent), and women were more likely to work in the informal sector. Although the law prohibits discrimination based on gender in employment and wages, the IBGE reported that in 2011 women received 72 percent of the income of men for comparable work.

Children

Birth Registration: Citizenship is derived from birth in the country or from a parent. According to 2010 IBGE census data, there were approximately 599,000 unregistered children nationwide. Without birth certificates children cannot be vaccinated or enrolled in school. If the problem persisted into adulthood, an unregistered adult could not obtain a worker's card or receive retirement benefits.

The CNJ, in partnership with the SDH, aimed to reduce the number of such children by registering children born in maternity wards. The National Documentation of Rural Workers initiative offered assistance in obtaining identification cards, birth certificates for children born in rural areas, labor cards, and tax documents. From 2004 to the end of 2012, more than 920,600 women and children had been documented through the program.

Child Abuse: Abuse and neglect of children and adolescents were problems and included rape, molestation, and impregnation of girls by family members. The SDH oversaw the National Program to Confront Sexual Violence against Children and Adolescents, which established nationwide strategies for combating child sexual abuse and best practices for treating victims.

From January to November, the SDH-operated Dial 100, a hotline for complaints of sexual abuse against children and adolescents, logged 35,140 complaints, compared with 19,946 during all of 2011. According to the SDH, the rise was due to increased national awareness of what constituted sexual abuse and sexual exploitation.

The NGO Social Service for Industry operated child protective centers in 21 cities in 17 states. The program served 3.5 million adolescents between the ages of 16 and 21, who received psychological counseling, medical attention, legal advice, and technical schooling.

According to data released by the National Register of Sheltered Children and the Public Ministry, there were approximately 45,600 children and adolescents living in 4,029 shelters provided by NGOs, churches, and other religious organizations throughout the country. The Public Ministry released data in August claiming that one-third of the sheltered children exceeded the two years they were allowed by law to reside in shelters and that 86 percent of children in shelters had families they could rejoin after two years.

The Death Threat Protection Program for Children and Adolescents brought in 1,501 children and adolescents and 2,230 families in 2011, the latest period for which data were available. A majority of those shielded by the program had received death threats due to involvement in drug trafficking, and most entered the program accompanied by one or more family members. The program offered psychological counseling and technical courses to reinsert these youth into stable community situations. The Index of Youth Homicides produced by the SDH and the UN Children's Fund (UNICEF) reported that homicides accounted for 45 percent of the deaths of adolescents between 12 and 18 years of age.

Forced and Early Marriage: The legal minimum age of marriage is 18 (age 16 with parental or legal representative consent). According to UNICEF, approximately 36 percent of women 20-24 years of age were married or in a union before age 18.

Sexual Exploitation of Children: The law sets a minimum age of 14 for consensual sex, with the penalty for statutory rape ranging from eight to15 years in prison. The country was a destination for child sex tourism. Several major coastal cities in the northeast served as tourist destinations for the sexual exploitation of children and adolescents. While no specific laws address child sex tourism, it is punishable under other criminal offenses. According to data from the SDH, University of

Brasilia, UNICEF, and ILO, more than 100,000 children were victims of sexual exploitation each year.

The SDH continued its national internet campaign against sexual abuse and sexual exploitation of children and adolescents. With a focus on prevention, the goal of the program was to raise awareness prior to the annual carnival season and the FIFA soccer World Cup.

The law criminalizes child pornography. The penalty for possession of child pornography is up to four years in prison and a fine. Those who produce, reproduce, or offer for sale child pornography or recruit a child to participate in a pornographic production may be imprisoned up to eight years and fined.

Although the country is not a large-scale producer of child pornography, such material was spread on social networking websites. The Public Ministry, Dial 100, and the NGO Safernet, in partnership with the Federal Police, registered 10,715 child pornography complaints between January 1 and July 1, compared with 19,311 complaints in the same period in 2011. From January to August, authorities imprisoned 41 individuals for disseminating child pornography on the internet.

The Ministry of Tourism continued to promote its code of conduct to prevent the commercial sexual exploitation of children in the tourism industry. The Federal Highway Police and the ILO continued to disseminate awareness materials in places such as gas stations, bars, restaurants, motels, and nightclubs along highways considered areas for sexual exploitation of children and adolescents. Despite these efforts, a Federal Highway Police study found 1,776 hotspots for child prostitution throughout the country, mainly at major highway intersections close to urban areas. The study also found that since 2006, the authorities had removed 3,812 children and adolescents from these hotspots and taken 1,662 individuals into custody for crimes against minors.

International Child Abductions: The country is a party to the 1980 Hague Convention on the Civil Aspects of International Child Abduction. For information see the Department of State's report on compliance at www.travel.state.gov/abduction/resources/congressreport/congressreport_4308.html as well as country-specific information at http://www.travel.state.gov/abduction/country/country_5886.html.

Anti-Semitism

According to the Jewish Federation, there were approximately 125,000 Jewish citizens, of whom approximately 65,000 were in the state of Sao Paulo and 40,000 in Rio de Janeiro state. It is illegal to write, edit, publish, or sell books that promote anti-Semitism or racism. The law enables courts to fine or imprison anyone who displays, distributes, or broadcasts anti-Semitic materials and mandates a two- to five-year prison term.

In the city of Sao Paulo, there were isolated incidents of anti-Semitism, including physical and verbal attacks against Jewish persons, anti-Semitic graffiti, and displays of neo-Nazism.

According to a study conducted by the State University of Campinas (Sao Paulo), neo-Nazi groups that traditionally operated in the southern states of Rio Grande do Sul, Santa Catarina, and Parana began to grow in the past decade in Federal District and Minas Gerais State. The study estimated that there were approximately 105,000 neo-Nazis in the three southern states and 29,000 in Sao Paulo state.

Trafficking in Persons

See the Department of State's *Trafficking in Persons Report* at www.state.gov/j/tip/.

Persons with Disabilities

The law prohibits discrimination against persons with physical and mental disabilities in employment, air travel and other transportation, education, and access to health care, and the federal government effectively enforced these provisions. An estimated 10 percent of the population had some form of disability. While federal and state laws mandate access to buildings for persons with disabilities, states did not enforce them effectively. A 1991 federal law requires private companies to hire disabled individuals at a minimum level of 2 percent of their workforce, but authorities did not effectively enforce this quota.

The National Council for the Rights of Persons with Disabilities and the National Council for the Rights of the Elderly, both within the SDH, have primary responsibility for promoting the rights of persons with disabilities. According to the SDH, specific problems included the short supply of affordable and up-to-date orthotics and prosthetics, scarcity of affordable housing with special adaptations, and a need for greater accessibility to public transport. Children with disabilities attended school (primary, secondary, and higher education), but there existed a shortage of schools with facilities for such persons. The absence of accessible infrastructure and schools had a significant impact within the workforce, and only an estimated 6 percent of the population with disabilities participated in the workforce.

The city government of Teresina, the state capital of Piaui, also funded infrastructure investments to improve mobility and access for the disabled community; it allocated roughly 1.7 million reais ($733,000) in public funds to improve city streets and sidewalks to make them more accessible for disabled persons.

The government improved access for persons with disabilities in its infrastructure development and in retrofitting public sports venues to prepare for the upcoming sporting events, including the 2016 Paralympics games.

National/Racial/Ethnic Minorities

The law prohibits racial discrimination, specifically the denial of public or private facilities, employment, or housing, to anyone based on race. The law also prohibits, and stipulates prison terms for, the incitement of racial discrimination or prejudice and the dissemination of racially offensive symbols and epithets. The 2010 census reported that for the first time white persons constituted less than half the population of 190.8 million, since a total of 99.7 million persons identified themselves as belonging to categories other than white. Despite laws and a high representation within the general population, darker-skinned citizens, particularly Afro-Brazilians, frequently encountered discrimination.

In August Teodoro Lalor de Lima, leader of a community of descendants of escaped slaves (quilombo), was stabbed to death in Belem, Para state. Lalor de Lima fought for the rights of quilombos and had received threats for his advocacy of quilombo communities' land rights. The Civil Police continued to investigate the killing.

Afro-Brazilians continued to be underrepresented in the government, professional positions, and middle and upper classes. They experienced a higher rate of unemployment and earned average wages below those of whites in similar positions. There was also a sizeable education gap. Afro-Brazilians were disproportionately negatively affected by crime, and black males were twice as likely as their white counterparts to be homicide victims.

The 2010 Racial Equality Statute continued to be controversial, due to its provision for nonquota affirmative action policies in education and employment. In 2012 the Supreme Court upheld racial quota systems at universities as constitutional, and a quotas law went into effect that gave the 59 federal universities four years to ensure that half of their incoming classes be from public schools, which generally served poorer students. Departments within the Federal University of Rio de Janeiro and the University of Brasilia also began to implement quotas for racial minorities in their master's and doctoral programs. Between 2001 and 2011, college attendance rates increased from 10 percent to 36 percent for black and mixed-race students ages 18 to 24.

In addition to the quota system, in May the Ministry of Education announced a stipend for students in federal universities who met certain income and racial requirements. Students from low income families earning less than 1,017 reais per month ($438) would be eligible to receive 400 reais ($172) per month, while students from indigenous and quilombo communities (communities of descendants of escaped slaves) could receive 900 reais ($388) per month.

Indigenous People

According to data from the National Indigenous Foundation (FUNAI), National Health Foundation, and the 2010 census, there were approximately 897,000 indigenous persons (0.5 percent of the national population), representing 305 distinct indigenous ethnic groups and 274 languages. Approximately 17,000 lived in 4,672 formally recognized indigenous zones, covering 12.5 percent of the national territory. Approximately 8 percent of the indigenous lands are concentrated in the Amazon region.

The law grants the indigenous population broad protection of their cultural patrimony, exclusive use of their traditional lands, and exclusive beneficial use of their territory. After consulting with the tribes involved, Congress must approve each request to exploit water resources, including ones with energy potential and minerals on indigenous lands. The law grants indigenous tribes rights to a portion of the profit resulting from mining. According to the constitution, all aboveground and underground minerals as well as hydroelectric-power potential belong to the government. The construction of the Belo Monte dam, one of the largest hydroelectric projects undertaken by the government, led to frequent conflicts with nearby indigenous communities. At times this resulted in conflict with security forces, which occasionally led to violence. The ILO and IACHR ruled that the project violated the government's international agreements on indigenous rights, and the UN Special Rapporteur on the Rights of Indigenous Peoples expressed similar concerns in his reporting.

The Maraiwatsede reserve, home to the Xavante indigenous group in the state of Mato Grosso, was demarcated in 1998, yet nonindigenous settlers continued to reside illegally in the reserve. While the 1988 constitution charged the federal government with demarcating indigenous areas within five years, the government had not completed the four phases of demarcation (identification, declaration, approval, and registration) by yearend. In August fires destroyed one-fifth of the Maraiwatsede reserve; some officials attributed the fires to soybean farmers and cattle ranchers taking revenge for their 2012 eviction from the lands.

In April a special commission began to analyze a constitutional amendment that would transfer the ability to demarcate indigenous territories from FUNAI to Congress, causing indigenous protesters to enter congressional hearings without permission at various times in the ensuing months. In May President Rousseff's chief of staff, Gleisi Hoffmann, stated that FUNAI did not have the capacity to mediate conflicts between indigenous people and rural landowners and that the government would explore including other government agencies in the decision-making process for demarcating indigenous lands. Since 2010 the government has cut funding to FUNAI by 67.8 percent to 5.9 million reais ($2.5million).

According to a June report released by the Indigenous Missionary Council, 60 indigenous persons were killed in 2012, 11 more than in 2011. In addition 1,054 indigenous persons suffered death threats and attempts on their lives. Mato Grosso do Sul state registered more than one-half of all indigenous homicides, with 37 deaths. Most of the violence against indigenous people was connected to contentious land demarcation disputes. For example, gunmen killed two indigenous persons in Mato Grosso do Sul in June. The Indigenous Missionary Council attributed the killings to the Guarani-Kaiowa peoples' desire to expand their territory, located on the border with Paraguay and next to three cattle ranches. According to the National Committee to Combat Rural Violence, an organization linked to the federal government, illegal evictions from demarcated lands by armed ranchers and farmers, often bearing forged documents, were among the main causes of violence against indigenous people.

Societal Abuses, Discrimination, and Acts of Violence Based on Sexual Orientation and Gender Identity

Federal law does not prohibit discrimination based on sexual orientation, but several states and municipalities have administrative regulations that prohibit such discrimination and provide for equal access to government services.

In June the SDH released its *Second Annual Report on Homophobic Violence*, which stated that in 2012 there were 315 LGBT-related homicides, compared with 278 in 2011. The NGO Rainbow Group considered the SDH report more accurate than the information in other annual reports on homophobic violence because of its use of government data as well as media reports.

According to the SDH, many transgender individuals had difficulty entering the formal labor market or study programs because an apparent discrepancy between the photograph on an individual's labor card and an individual's personal appearance prevented some from obtaining permission to work.

The National LGBT Council, created in 2010 to combat discrimination and promote the rights of LGBT people, continued to meet every two months. Meetings were open to the public and broadcast over the internet. During the year the SDH launched the National System to Promote LGBT Rights and Confront Violence against LGBT Persons, with the purpose of promoting public policies to mitigate discrimination affecting the LGBT community. In August the states of Goias, Minas Gerais, and Rio Grande do Sul began registering cases of homophobic violence.

A 1999 resolution of the Federal Council of Psychology prohibited psychological professionals from offering services that treated homosexuality as a mental illness. Federal Deputy Marco Feliciano, president of the Chamber of Deputies' Human Rights and Minorities Commission, sparked controversy by supporting legislation that would lift these restrictions and allow psychological professionals to offer treatment to homosexual patients seeking to reorient their sexuality. The Chamber of Deputies blocked the proposed law.

On June 4, Rio de Janeiro's state-run program "Rio without Homophobia" began a second round of diversity training for police officers, focusing on the rights of LGBT persons. Five thousand officers stationed in the city of Rio participated in the first training session.

The state of Pernambuco sponsored a "human rights road show" program, the first of its kind in the country. The road show visits often led to increased reporting of crimes against the LGBT community. On June 25, the governor of Pernambuco signed a decree creating a data center to register statistics on cases of homophobic violence in the state. The center was required to record and report every 12 months all information on cases of violence against the LGBT community.

Other Societal Violence or Discrimination

Sao Paulo Governor Geraldo Alckmin announced an involuntary drug treatment program on January 11, in response to the rising use of crack cocaine and the spread of drug markets known as "cracolandias," where addicts consumed the drug openly on the streets. The new program allowed state health workers or family members of addicts in "advanced stages" of addiction and at risk of death to recommend court-ordered treatment without the consent of the patient. A judge and a state-appointed doctor would then decide whether to commit patients to treatment centers. According to a Federal University of Sao Paulo study, there were more than one million crack cocaine users in the country.

Violence connected to environmental activism and agrarian conflicts continued. According to the Catholic NGO Pastoral Land Commission, 36 individuals lost their lives in killings linked to land- and water-rights conflicts that occurred in remote areas in 2012, a 24 percent increase from 2011. Seventeen of the killings occurred in the north, including nine in the state of Rondonia.

In August a judge in Minas Gerais state ordered four men implicated in the killings of five land reform activists to be placed in preventive custody. The judge handed down the order due to threats against potential jury members and witnesses as well as repeated efforts by the defense lawyer to delay the trial. The case continued at year's end.

On May 14, the Supreme Court overturned the conviction of Vitalmiro Bastos de Moura, accused of ordering the 2005 murder of Catholic nun Dorothy Mae Stang, and ordered a fourth trial after determining Moura's lawyer lacked sufficient time to prepare his defense. On September 19, the court again convicted Moura of ordering the murder of Dorothy Stang and sentenced him to 30 years in prison. In July, Rayfran das Neves Sales, the gunman who killed Dorothy Stang, was released from prison on parole after serving eight years of his 27-year sentence.

There were no reported cases of societal violence or discrimination against persons with HIV/AIDS.

Section 7. Worker Rights

a. Freedom of Association and the Right to Collective Bargaining

The law provides for freedom of association for all workers (except members of the military, uniformed police, and firefighters) but limits organizing at the enterprise level and imposes a mandatory union tax on workers and employers. The law provides for the right to strike except for the armed forces, military police, and firefighters. Civil police are allowed to conduct strikes. The law prohibits antiunion discrimination, including the dismissal of employees who are candidates for, or holders of, union leadership positions, and it requires employers to reinstate workers fired for union activity.

New unions must register with the MTE, which accepts the registration unless objections are filed by other unions. The law stipulates certain restrictions, such as "unicidade" (in essence one union per city), which limits freedom of association by prohibiting multiple, competing unions of the same professional category in a given geographical area. Unions that represent workers in the same geographical area and professional category may contest registration. If the objection is found to be valid, the MTE does not register the union. While a number of competing unions existed, the MTE and courts enforced unicidade in decisions regarding the registration of new unions. Most elements of the labor movement and the International Trade Union Confederation criticized unicidade.

The law stipulates that a strike may be ruled "abusive" by labor courts and be punishable if a number of conditions are not met, such as maintaining essential services during a strike, notifying employers at least 48 hours before the beginning of a walkout, and ending a strike after a labor court decision. Employers may not hire substitute workers during a legal strike or fire workers for strike-related activity, provided the strike is not ruled abusive.

The law obliges a union to negotiate on behalf of all registered workers in the professional category and geographical area it represents, regardless of whether an employee pays voluntary membership dues. The law permits the government to reject clauses of collective bargaining agreements that conflict with government policy. Collective bargaining is effectively prohibited in the public sector; the constitution allows it, but implementing legislation had not been enacted.

Authorities at times did not effectively enforce laws protecting freedom of association and collective bargaining. Penalties under the law ranging from 10 reais to 1,000 reais ($4.31 to $431) were generally sufficient to deter violations, and labor courts enforced payments. Parties generally agreed that the courts decided cases fairly.

Freedom of association was generally respected. Collective bargaining was widespread in formal sector establishments of the private sector. Worker organizations were independent of the government and political parties, and there was no government interference in union activities. Intimidation and killings of rural union organizers and their agents continued. For example, on March 21, an unidentified assailant shot and killed Fatima Benites, president of the Union of Workers and Rural Workers of Bela Vista, Mato Grosso do Sul, close to the union headquarters.

Employers fired strike organizers for reasons ostensibly unrelated to strikes. Legal recourse related to retaliatory discharge, although improving, was often a protracted process.

b. Prohibition of Forced or Compulsory Labor

The labor law prohibits what it calls "slave labor," defined as "reducing someone to a condition analogous to slavery," including subjecting someone to forced labor as well to exploitative working conditions in general, such as long workdays, unhygienic work conditions, extremely arduous labor, and labor performed in degrading working conditions. The government took a number of actions to enforce the law, although forced labor continued to occur in a number of states. Violators of forced labor laws face sentences of up to eight years in prison. The law also provides penalties for various crimes related to forced labor, such as recruiting or transporting workers or obliging them to incur debt as part of a forced labor scheme.

The National Commission to Eradicate Slave Labor coordinated government efforts to combat forced and exploitative labor and provided a forum for input from civil society. During 2012, the latest year for which such data were available, the MTE reported removing 2,428 laborers from "conditions analogous to slavery" in 164 unannounced inspections of 331properties. The government uses the terms "slave labor" and "conditions analogous to slavery" under the broader definition of forced or poor labor conditions. It was unclear how many of these cases involved forced labor as opposed to degrading labor conditions.

The MTE's Mobile Inspection Unit teams conducted surprise inspections of properties on which forced labor was suspected or reported, using teams composed of labor inspectors, labor prosecutors from the Federal Labor Prosecutor's Office, and Federal Police officers. Mobile teams levied fines on landowners who used forced labor and required employers to provide back pay and benefits to workers before returning the workers to their municipalities of origin. Workers removed by mobile units were entitled to three months' salary at the minimum wage. The MTE ordered employers to pay 9.9 million reais ($4.27 million) in back pay in 2012. Few specialized services were provided to these workers, and NGOs noted a high revictimization rate.

The government continued to partner with the ILO in projects to eradicate forced labor and promote decent work in the states of Mato Grosso, Bahia, and Sao Paulo.

The MTE also published a "dirty list" to expose publicly employers (persons or legal entities) caught using forced labor. The list was updated every six months by the MTE's Secretariat of Labor Inspections and was available on the MTE website. Inclusion on the "dirty list" had serious financial consequences in that public financial institutions as well as many private banks deny credit and other services to listed individuals and companies. As of November the list contained 488 names.

During the year the Sao Paulo state government approved legislation to combat forced and exploitative labor in supply chains. The law provides for a 10-year revocation of the business license of any entity that directly or indirectly employs workers under forced labor conditions.

Efforts against forced labor were hindered by failure to impose effective penalties, the remoteness of the area where the crime typically occurred, lack of awareness of rights, delays in judicial procedure that resulted in de facto impunity for those responsible, and lack of sufficient programs to assist victims of forced labor. Accurate, nationwide statistics on prosecutions for forced labor cases were not available. In September a federal court in Sao Paulo sentenced Ronaldo Perao to seven years and six months in prison for subjecting 21 employees to "conditions analogous to slavery" on his coffee plantation in 2011. The defendant was not imprisoned and planned to appeal the conviction.

Efforts of the federal government were supported by a number of state initiatives, and several states have state commissions for the eradication of forced labor, including Tocantins, Bahia, Rio de Janeiro, Sao Paulo, Mato Grosso do Sul, Para, Maranhao, Mato Grosso, and Rio Grande do Sul. The Sao Paulo State Commission for the Eradication of Forced Labor (COETRAE) met regularly during the year under the coordination of the Secretariat of Justice. The commission, created in September 2011, functioned in tandem with the Sao Paulo Nucleus to Combat Trafficking in Persons. COETRAE was composed of members from the Secretariats of Justice, Labor, Agriculture, Environment, Treasury, and Education and also from the Public Ministry, police forces, and NGOs. The commission focused exclusively on cases of forced labor as well as what the law terms "conditions analogous to slavery."

On March 14, nine members of the Mato Grosso state COETRAE left the commission due to the perceived ineffectiveness of the organization. In a letter signed by various commission participants including unions, the Pastoral Land Commission, judges, and the Federal Public Ministry, among others, the former members complained of frequent cancellations of meetings, the lack of an updated State Pan to Eradicate Forced Labor, and comments made by Mato Grosso government officials questioning the validity of MTE's "dirty list."

Forced labor, including by children, occurred in many states, in work such as clearing forest to provide cattle pastureland, logging, charcoal production, raising livestock, and other agricultural activities. Forced labor often involved young men drawn from the less-developed northeastern states – Maranhao, Piaui, Tocantins, Para, and Ceara – and the central state of Goias to work in the northern and central-western regions of the country. In addition there were reports of forced labor in the construction industry also involving young men principally from the northeast. Cases of forced labor were also reported in sweatshops in the city of Sao Paulo; the victims were often from neighboring countries, particularly Bolivia and Paraguay. In August labor inspectors removed 13 Bolivian workers and four children from a sweatshop in Sao Paulo where they worked for upwards of 13 hours a day and were forced to live where they worked. In 2012 the Pernambuco Labor Prosecutor's Office found and removed 33 workers in forced labor conditions; 21 of them worked in sugar mills and six in the construction industry.

The coordinator of the National Campaign to Combat Slave Labor (linked to the Public Ministry of Labor) estimated that there were between 20,000 and 50,000 laborers working in "conditions analogous to slavery" at any given time during the year. According to the Pastoral Land Commission's 2012 report published in May, there were 168 incidents in which people were found in "conditions analogous to slavery." States with the highest number of removed workers were Mato Grosso, Goias, Amapa, Para, Maranhao, and Tocantins. The primary economic activities where forced labor was found included ranching, charcoal making, and farming. Forced labor in domestic servitude involving women and adolescents (the latter typically working with their parents) was also reported.

Also see the Department of State's *Trafficking in Persons Report* at www.state.gov/j/tip/.

c. Prohibition of Child Labor and Minimum Age for Employment

The minimum working age is 16 years, and apprenticeships may begin at age 14. The law bars all minors under age 18 from work that constitutes a physical strain or occurs in unhealthy, dangerous, or morally harmful conditions. Hazardous work includes an extensive list of activities within 13 occupational categories, including domestic service, garbage scavenging, and fertilizer production. The law requires parental permission for minors to work as apprentices.

The MTE is responsible for inspecting worksites to enforce child labor laws. Penalties for violations ranged from 402 reais to 2,013 reais ($173 to $868), doubling for a second violation and tripling for a third, and were sufficient to deter violations and were generally enforced; however, NGOs asserted that fines were usually too small to serve as an effective deterrent. Most inspections of children in the workplace were driven by complaints brought by workers, teachers, unions, NGOs, and the media. Labor inspectors remained unable to enter private homes and farms, where much of the nation's child labor occurred.

The government implemented innovative programs to prevent child labor, including the Program to Eradicate Child Labor (PETI), coordinated by the Ministry of Social Development and Combating Hunger with state and local authorities. Through PETI, families with children seven to 15 years of age working in selected hazardous activities received monthly cash stipends to keep their children in school. PETI serviced more than 820,000 children in 3,500 municipalities. Also through the ministry, the Bolsa Familia program provided a monthly stipend to low-income families that kept their children up to age 17 in school and met certain child health requirements. The Bolsa Familia served more than 13 million households nationwide. Beyond the Bolsa Familia, the government operated the Brasil Sem Miseria (Brazil without Misery) and Brasil Carinhoso (Caring Brazil) programs to build on programs such as the Bolsa

Familia as well as to provide access to public services and to stimulate employment opportunities. The government also continued to partner with the ILO in projects to eradicate child labor in the state of Mato Grosso. The Federal Police also expended funds to respond to criminal cases involving forced child labor.

Nevertheless, child labor continued to be a problem. The 2011 IBGE National Household Survey, reflecting the most recent data available, showed that 4.28 million of an estimated 44 million children between the ages of five and 17 were engaged in some form of child labor, more than 250,000 of whom were domestic workers. Of the minors engaged in child labor, children between the ages of five and nine made up 2 percent of the child labor population, children 10 to 14 made up 27.5 percent, and children 15 to 17 made up 70.5 percent. According to 2010 data from the MTE, the majority of the children were employed in street vending (42 percent), followed by automobile washing (10 percent), manufacturing (8 percent), and agriculture (3 percent).

According to a study conducted by the daily newspaper *Folha de Sao Paulo* and based on 2010 census data, the incidence of child labor was more prevalent in the north, where one in 10 children worked, either in paid or unpaid jobs. The 2010 census reported that 132,000 children between the ages 10 and 14 were the sole providers for their families. Approximately one-half of child laborers received no income, and 90 percent worked in the unregistered informal sector. Slightly more than one-half of child laborers worked in rural areas. The study also found that 95 percent of the children who worked also attended school.

According to MTE data, 5,000 children and adolescents were found in situations that violated minimum-age laws in 6,387 unannounced inspections from January to September. A majority, 81 percent, of those found were young boys. In 2012 a total of 7,393 inspections discovered 7,124 children and adolescents employed in violation of minimum-age laws.

Children worked in agriculture, including in raising livestock and in the production of cashews, coffee, sugarcane, cotton, manioc, pineapple, sisal, soybeans, rice, and tobacco. Children were also involved in the production of ceramics, bricks, charcoal, and footwear.

Also see the Department of Labor's *Findings on the Worst Forms of Child Labor* at www.dol.gov/ilab/programs/ocft/tda.htm.

d. Acceptable Conditions of Work

In January the minimum wage increased to 678 reais ($292) per month. According to 2010 IBGE data, the most recent information available, the per capita income of approximately 50 percent of the population was below the minimum wage. IGBE data also revealed that 8.5 percent of inhabitants (16.2 million) were considered "extremely poor" or earning less than 70 reais ($30) per month.

The law limits the work week to 44 hours and specifies a weekly rest period of 24 consecutive hours, preferably on Sundays. The law also provides for paid annual vacation, prohibits excessive compulsory overtime, limits overtime to two hours per workday, and stipulates that hours worked above the monthly limit must be compensated with at least time-and-a-half pay; these provisions generally were enforced for all groups of workers in the formal sector.

The MTE sets occupational, health, and safety standards that are consistent with internationally recognized norms, although unsafe working conditions were prevalent throughout the country, especially in construction. Accidents at large construction projects for the FIFA soccer World Cup, such as stadiums and infrastructure, prompted slightly improved enforcement of safety regulations. The law requires employers to establish internal committees for accident prevention in workplaces. It also provides for the protection of employees from being fired for their committee activities.

As part of its efforts to combat forced labor, the MTE's Mobile Inspection Unit teams also addressed issues related to acceptable conditions of work such as long workdays and unsafe or unhygienic work conditions. At the end of 2012, the MTE employed a total of 2,995 labor inspectors, slightly down from 3,085 at the end of 2011. Penalties for violations included fines and were generally enforced. In March the MTE announced the creation of the National Labor Inspection School for the training of labor inspectors throughout the country.

In August labor inspectors removed 40 workers from an orange plantation in the interior of Sao Paulo state. The landowner subjected the workers to long work days, insufficient salaries, and degrading living conditions. One pair of workers lived in a converted chicken coop. The landowner owed each worker 20,000 reais ($8,620) as well as the cost of transportation back to their cities of origin.

Irregularities in the work conditions of Bolivian immigrants working in the garment industry, principally in Sao Paulo, continued in 2012. In July, 28 labor inspectors removed Bolivian immigrant workers from degrading work conditions in a sweatshop in Sao Paulo run by textile manufacturing company Restoque, which produced clothes for the popular Le Lis Blanc and Bourgeois Boheme brands. The company signed an agreement with the Public Ministry of Labor to change its labor practices as well as pay one million reais ($431,000) for moral damages that could keep Restoque off the "dirty list." The company complied immediately with the agreement and said that the sweatshops in question were run by a third-party contractor.

According to IBGE data, there were approximately 44.2 million persons in the informal sector in 2011, the most recent year for which data were available. Most unregistered workers were in the agricultural sector. Not all foreign migrant workers, informal sector workers, and unregistered workers were subject to hazardous working conditions, but these groups were at a higher risk of being subjected to exploitative conditions.

In 2012 there were approximately 724,000 workplace accidents and 2,731 workplace fatalities. On October 1, the Labor Court halted construction at the Arena da Baixada stadium in Curitiba, one of the sites set to host World Cup games in 2014. Judge Lorraine Colnago found conditions at the stadium to be dangerous for workers and fined the Brazilian Football League reais ($215,500) per day for failure to comply with labor laws.